Presented

_____

From:

_____

Date:

_____

FAMOUS OLD DEAD GUYS

Classic Quotation Collection

HONOR **HB** BOOKS

Inspiration and Motivation for the Seasons of Life

COOK COMMUNICATIONS MINISTRIES
Colorado Springs, Colorado • Paris, Ontario
KINGSWAY COMMUNICATIONS LTD
Eastbourne, England

Honor® is an imprint of
Cook Communications Ministries, Colorado Springs, CO 80918
Cook Communications, Paris, Ontario
Kingsway Communications, Eastbourne, England

FAMOUS OLD DEAD GUYS: CLASSIC QUOTATION COLLECTION
© 2005 by Honor Books

First Printing, 2005
Printed in Canada

Printing/Year
10 9 8 7 6 5 4 3 2 1 / 05 06 07 08 09

Manuscript compiled by Shanna Gregor, Scripture quotations marked NIV taken from the HOLY BIBLE, NEW INTERNATIONAL VERSION®. Copyright © 1973, 1978, 1984 International Bible Society. Used by permission of Zondervan. All rights reserved. Scripture quotations marked NASB taken from the New American Standard Bible®, Copyright © 1960, 1962, 1963, 1968, 1971, 1972, 1973, 1975, 1977, 1995 by The Lockman Foundation. Used by permission. (www.Lockman.org.) Scriptures quotations marked KJV are from the King James Version of the Bible. (Public Domain.) Scripture quotations marked NKJV™ are taken from the New King James Version®. Copyright © 1982 by Thomas Nelson, Inc. Used by permission. All rights reserved. Scripture quotations marked AMP taken from the Amplified® Bible, Copyright © 1954, 1958, 1962, 1964, 1965, 1987 by The Lockman Foundation. Used by permission. (www.Lockman.org) Scripture quotations marked AMP are taken from *The Message*. Copyright © 1993, 1994, 1995, 1996, 2000, 2001, 2002. Used by permission of NavPress Publishing Group. Scripture quotations marked NLT are taken from the Holy Bible, New Living Translation, copyright © 1996. Used by permission of Tyndale House Publishers, Inc., Wheaton, Illinois 60189. All rights reserved.

ISBN: 1562927299

The reasonable thing is to learn from those who can teach.

—Sophocles

The things that are closest to our hearts are the things we talk about, and if God is close to your heart, you will talk about him.

—A. W. Tozer

Let love and faithfulness never leave you; bind them around your neck, write them on the tablet of your heart.

Proverbs 3:3 NIV

Knowing God

Andrew Murray

There are two ways of knowing things. The one is in the mind by notion or conception: I know about something. The other is in the life: I know by inward experience. The mind can form thoughts about God from the Bible and know all the doctrines of salvation, while the inner life doesn't know God's power to save (1 John 4:8). He may know all about God's love and be able to utter beautiful things about it. But unless he loves, he doesn't know God. Only love can know God. The knowledge of God is life eternal.

 he soul of the diligent shall
be made rich.

Proverbs 13:4 NKJV

*B*e active, be diligent. Avoid laziness, sloth, indolence. Fly from every degree, every appearance of it; else you will never be more than half a Christian.

—John Wesley

Look! Look!

Charles Spurgeon

He [the speaker] knew me to be a stranger. Just fixing his eyes on me, as if he knew all my heart, he said, "Young man, you look very miserable."

Well, I did, but I had not been accustomed to have remarks made from the pulpit on my personal appearance before. However, it was a good blow, struck right home. He continued, "And you always will be miserable—miserable in life, and miserable in death—if you don't obey my text; but if you obey now, this moment, you will be saved."

Then, lifting up his hands, he shouted, "Young man, look to Jesus Christ. Look! Look! Look! You have nothin' to do but to look and live."

I saw at once the way of salvation... when I heard that word, "Look!" What a charming word it seemed to me! Oh! I looked until I could almost have looked my eyes away.

The cloud was gone, the darkness had rolled away, and that moment I saw the sun; and I could have risen that instant, and sung with the most enthusiastic of them, of the precious blood of Christ, and the simple faith which looks alone to HIM.

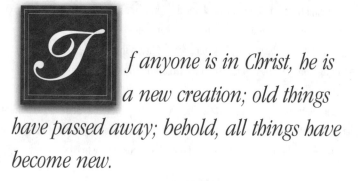 *f anyone is in Christ, he is a new creation; old things have passed away; behold, all things have become new.*

2 Corinthians 5:17 NKJV

*W*hen by the Spirit of God, I understood these words, "The just shall live by faith," I
felt born again like a new man. I entered through the open doors
into the very Paradise of God!
—Martin Luther

*G*od salvages the individual by liquidating him and then raising
him again to newness of life.
—A. W. Tozer

*C*hrist himself is my righteousness. I look at him as a gift to me, in himself;
so that in him I have all things.
—Martin Luther

Faith is the assurance (the confirmation, the title deed) of the things [we] hope for, being the proof of things [we] do not see and the conviction of their reality [faith perceiving as real fact what is not revealed to the senses].

Hebrews 11:1 AMP

Now I have found the ground wherein
Sure my soul's anchor may remain—
The wounds of Jesus, for my sin
Before the world's foundation slain;
Whose mercy shall unshaken stay,
When heaven and earth are fled away.

—F. B. Meyer

Faith—An Artist

John Bunyan

Faith receiveth the promise, embraceth it, and comforteth the soul unspeakably with it.
Faith is so great an artist in arguing and reasoning with the soul, that it will
bring over the hardest heart that it hath to deal with.
It will bring to my remembrance at once, both my vileness against God, and his goodness
towards me; it will show me, that though I deserve not to breathe in the air,
yet that God will have me an heir of glory.

 *he deeper your love, the higher it goes; every cloud is a flag to your faithfulness.*

Psalm 57:10 MSG

The more a person loves, the closer he approaches the image of God.

Spending the Lord's Money

John Wesley

If a doubt should arise in your mind concerning what you should spend on yourself or your family, calmly inquire:

1) In expending this sum, am I acting according to my character? Am I acting as a steward of my Lord's goods?

2) Am I doing this in obedience to his Word?

3) Can I offer up this action as a sacrifice to God through Jesus Christ?

4) Have I reason to believe that for this I shall have a reward at the resurrection of the just?

The Test of Prosperity

Charles Spurgeon

The unsoundness of a vessel is not seen when it is empty. When it is filled with water, then we will see whether or not it leaks. Likewise, it is during times of prosperity that we are tested. Men do not fully discover what they are really like until they are tried by the fullness of success.

Praise finds pride, wealth reveals selfishness, and triumph exposes the leak of unbelief. Success is the crucible of character…. O Lord, preserve us when we are full as much as when we are empty.

*indicate me, O LORD, for I have led a blameless life; I have trusted in the LORD without wavering. Test me, O LORD, and try me, examine my heart and my mind; for your love is ever before me, and I walk continually in your truth.*

Psalm 26:1–3 NIV

*T*he only guide to man is his conscience; the only shield to his memory is the rectitude and sincerity of his actions. It is very imprudent to walk through life without this shield, because we are so often mocked by the failure of our hopes and the upsetting of our calculations; but with this shield, however the fates may play, we march always in the ranks of honor.

—Winston Churchill

*N*othing makes a man so virtuous as belief of the truth. A lying doctrine will soon beget a lying practice. A man cannot have an erroneous belief without by-and-by having an erroneous life. I believe the one thing naturally begets the other.

—Charles Spurgeon

*R*ather than love, than money, than fame, give me truth.

—Henry David Thoreau

Grace is but glory begun, and glory is but grace perfected.
—Jonathan Edwards

Even the righteousness of God through faith in Jesus Christ for all those who believe; for there is no distinction; for all have sinned and fall short of the glory of God, being justified as a gift by His grace through the redemption which is in Christ Jesus.

Romans 3:22– 24 NASB

Grace for Each Day

D. L. Moody

The Israelites used to gather fresh manna every day; they were not allowed to store it up. There is a lesson here for us. If we would be strong and vigorous, we must go to God daily. A man can no more take in a supply of grace for the future than he can eat enough today to last him for the next six months, or take sufficient air into his lungs at once to sustain life for a week to come. We must draw upon God's boundless stores of grace from day to day as we need it.

*nd let us not grow weary while doing good, for in due season we shall reap if we do not lose heart.*

Galatians 6:9 NKJV

*A*dversity has ever been considered the state in which a man most easily becomes acquainted with himself.
—Samuel Johnson

Abraham Believed God

E.W. Bullinger

We have the essence of the gospel of God, and of his grace. That gospel is explained in Romans 1:1 to be the "Gospel of God." God's Good News; and faith cometh by hearing it. This is the gospel that Abraham believed; he believed God; believed what God said. The patriarch's feet were firmly planted on God's ground; his eyes were fixed on God himself. He had no shadow of doubt as to his possessing, in due time, all that God had promised. He did not hope it, still less did he doubt it, or go on asking for what God said he had given. Faith must have respect to a promise not to a feeling. True faith rests on the testimony of God's Word. No doubt it is by the gracious energy of the Holy Spirit that any one can exercise this living faith, but we are speaking now of the true ground of faith, the authority for faith, the basis on which alone it can rest, and that surely is the Word of God, which is able to make wise unto salvation without any human intervention whatsoever.

*n him [Jesus Christ] we have redemption through his blood, the forgiveness of sins, in accordance with the riches of God's grace that he lavished on us with all wisdom and understanding.*

Ephesians 1:7–8 NIV

*F*orgiveness ought to be like a canceled note—torn in two and burned up,
so that it can never be shown against one.

—Henry Ward Beecher

*L*ord, make me a channel of your peace. Where there is hatred, let me bring love.
Where there is offense, forgiveness. Where there is discord, reconciliation.
Where there is doubt, faith. Where there is despair, hope.
Where there is sadness, joy. Where there is darkness, your light.
If we give, we are made rich. If we forget ourselves, we find peace.
If we forgive, we receive forgiveness. If we die, we receive eternal resurrection.
Give us peace, Lord.

—St. Francis of Assisi

*R*ead the Bible as if you were seeking for something of great value. It is a good deal better to take a single chapter and spend a month on it than to read the Bible at random for a month.

—D. L. Moody

*Y*our word is a lamp to my feet and a light to my path.

Psalm 119:105 NKJV

Feeding on the Word
Charles Spurgeon

An old man once said, "For a long period of time, I puzzled myself about the difficulties of Scripture until at last I came to the conclusion that reading the Bible was like eating fish. When I find a difficulty, I set it aside and call it a bone. Why should I choke on the bone when there is so much nutritious meat for me? Someday, perhaps, I may find that even the bone will give me nourishment."

Dear Christian, do not become discouraged and disheartened at the parts of the Bible you do not understand. Simply move on, believing that one day God will open your mind to his deeper, more puzzling truths. In the meantime, grab hold of the morsels you do comprehend and feast on the banquet set before you.

Your Mission

Andrew Murray

It is a great help if an ambassador knows clearly what his mission is, that he has nothing to do but accomplish it and that he has given himself undividedly to do this one thing. For the Christian, it is no less important that he should know that he has a mission, what its nature is, and how he is to accomplish it.

Every Christian must be the image of Jesus... that the world may know what Christ is like. Whoever you are and wherever you live, the Lord has chosen you to be his representative in the circle in which you move.

He has fixed his heart on you and saved you, in order that you will exhibit to those around you the very image of his unseen glory.

The Lord does not demand anything that he does not give the power to perform. Every believer may depend on it, that as the Father gave his Holy Spirit to the Son to fulfill his mission, so Jesus will give his people all the power and wisdom they need.

*t is God who arms me with strength, and makes my way perfect.*

Psalm 18:32 NKJV

*H*e is greatest whose strength carries up the most hearts by the attraction of his own.
—Henry Ward Beecher

*T*he strength of a man's virtue should not be measured by his special exertions,
but by his habitual acts.
—Blaise Pascal

*N*othing is so strong as gentleness and nothing is so gentle as real strength.
—Ralph W. Sockman

The function of prayer is not to influence God, but rather to change
the nature of the one who prays.

—Sören Kierkegaard

The LORD has heard my supplication, the LORD receives my prayer.
Psalm 6:9 NASB

Early Prayer

E. M. Bounds

The men who have done the most for God in this world have been early on their knees. He who fritters away the early morning, its opportunity and freshness, in other pursuits than seeking God will make poor headway seeking him the rest of the day.

If God is not first in our thoughts and efforts in the morning, he will be in the last place the remainder of the day.

Behind this early rising and early praying is the ardent desire which presses us into this pursuit after God.

e strong and take heart, all you who hope in the LORD.

Psalm 31:24 NIV

*H*ope means hoping when things are hopeless, or it is no virtue at all.... As long as matters are really hopeful, hope is mere flattery or platitude; it is only when everything is hopeless that hope begins to be a strength.

—G. K. Chesterton

The Engrafted Word

A. B. Simpson

The principle of grafting is very simple and suggestive. On a common root or stock a cultivated bud or branch is fastened, and trained to grow into its new trunk and stem until all its vegetable organism has become connected with the new fountain head. And then it begins to bear, not the fruit of the old stem, which is but a common crab or wild vine, but the cultivated fruit in all its mellowness and delicacy of flavor. It is really drawing upon the life of the old root, but crowning it with new beauty and richest fruitfulness.

Upon the stem of our natural life God engrafts his Word, and so infuses and in-works that Word into our very life that it becomes the element of our being and the second nature of all our habits, controlling us without arbitrary constraint and making it our delight to do his will.

We do right because we want to. We serve God because we love him. Obedience becomes as natural as sin was before, and the heart is spontaneous and free in all its spiritual affections and actions. Obedience, therefore, is not a matter of outward authority, but inward impulse.

*o not conform any longer to the pattern of this world, but be transformed by the renewing of your mind. Then you will be able to test and approve what God's will is—his good, pleasing and perfect will.*

Romans 12:2 NIV

The best way to control our thoughts is to offer the mind to God in
complete surrender.
—A. W. Tozer

Write down the thoughts of the moment. Those that come unsought
for are commonly the most valuable.
—Francis Bacon

Guard your roving thoughts with a jealous care, for speech is but the dialer of
thoughts, and every fool can plainly read in your words what
is the hour of your thoughts.
—Alfred Lord Tennyson

The dear angels are not so proud as we human beings are. They walk in obedience to God, serve mankind, and take care of little children. How could they perform a more significant work than taking care of children day and night?

—Martin Luther

Behold, children are a gift of the LORD.
Psalm 127:3 NASB

Discipline Early

Charles Spurgeon

With children, you must mix gentleness with firmness. They must not always have their own way, but they must not always be thwarted. Give to a pig when it grunts and to a child when it cries, and you will have a fine pig and a spoiled child.

Unless we look well to it, our children will be a nuisance to others and a torment to us. If we never have headaches through rebuking our little children, we will have plenty of heartaches when they grow up.

*e [the Lord] reached down from heaven and rescued me; he drew me out of deep waters.*

Psalm 18:16 NLT

Despair of ever being saved, "except thou be born again," or of seeing God "without holiness," or of having part in Christ except thou "love him above father, mother, or thy own life." This kind of despair is one of the first steps to heaven.

—Richard Baxter

The Blessed Life

F. B. Meyer

There is a Christian life which, on comparison with that experienced by the majority of Christians, is as summer to winter, or, as the mature fruitfulness of a golden autumn to the struggling promise of a cold and late spring.

And the blessedness of this blessed life lies in this: that we trust the Lord to do in us and for us what we could not do. And we find that he does not belie his Word, but that, according to our faith, so it is done to us. The weary spirit, which has vainly sought to realize its ideal by its own strivings and efforts, now gives itself over to the strong and tender hands of the Lord Jesus, and he accepts the task, and at once begins to work in it to will and to do of his own good pleasure, delivering it from the tyranny of besetting sin, and fulfilling in it his own perfect ideal.

The blessed should be the normal life of every Christian—in work and rest, in the building up of the inner life, and in the working out of the life-plan. It is God's thought not for a few, but for all his children.

 *y humility and the fear of the Lord are riches and honor and life.*

Proverbs 22:4 NKJV

*H*umility is the foundation of all the other virtues hence, in the soul in which this virtue does not exist there cannot be any other virtue except in mere appearance.

—St. Augustine

*H*umility is to make a right estimate of one's self.

—Charles Spurgeon

*T*he churches must learn humility as well as teach it.

—George Bernard Shaw

The Lord has made his revelation known to the world, and it is up to you and not to the Lord. He has done all he ever will or can do to save this world. he has given sunshine and rain and ground; it is up to you to plant the seed, to plow it or starve to death.

God has done his part; he will do no more.

—Billy Sunday

The fruit of the righteous is a tree of life, and he who wins souls is wise.

Proverbs 11:30 NKJV

Soul Winning

Billy Sunday

It is the simplest and most effective work in the world. Andrew wins Peter; Peter turns around and wins three thousand at Pentecost.

Years ago a man went into a shoe store in Boston and found a young fellow selling shoes and boots. He talked to him about Jesus Christ and won him for Christ. The name of that little boy was Dwight L. Moody. Do you know the name of the man who won Moody for Christ? His name was Kimball. God used Kimball to win Moody, but he used Moody to win the multitude.

s we have opportunity, let us do good to all.

Galatians 6:10 NIV

*P*eople are always blaming their circumstances for what they are. I don't believe in circumstances. The people who get on in this world are the people who get up and look for the circumstances they want, and, if they can't find them, make them.

—George Bernard Shaw

Seize God-given Opportunities

D. L. Moody

A sculptor once showed a visitor his studio. It was full of statues of gods. One sculpture in particular the visitor found very curious—the face was concealed with hair, and there were wings on each foot.

"What is his name?" said the visitor.

"Opportunity," was the reply.

"Why is his face hidden?"

"Because men seldom know him when he comes to them," the sculptor said.

"Why has he wings on his feet?"

"Because he is soon gone," the artist answers, "and once gone, can never be overtaken."

It becomes us, then, to make the most of the opportunities God has given us. It depends a good deal on ourselves what our future shall be. We can sow for a good harvest—or we can do like the Sioux Indians who, when the United States Commissioner of Indian Affairs sent them a supply of grain for sowing, ate it up. Men are constantly sacrificing their eternal future to the passing enjoyment of the present moment; they fail or neglect to recognize the dependence of the future upon the present. God sends us opportunities; it is up to us to seize them.

*et the LORD longs to be gracious to you; he rises to show you compassion. For the LORD is a God of justice. Blessed are all who wait for him!*

Isaiah 30:18 NIV

*K*ind words produce their own image in men's souls; and a beautiful image it is. They soothe and quiet and comfort the hearer. They shame him out of his sour, morose, unkind feelings. We have not yet begun to use kind words in such abundance as they ought to be used.

—Blaise Pascal

*M*an may dismiss compassion from his heart, but God never will.

—William Cowper

*T*he purpose of human life is to serve, and to show compassion and the will to help others.

—Albert Schweitzer

When it is a question of God's almighty Spirit, never say, "I can't."
—Oswald Chambers

I have strength for all things in Christ Who empowers me [I am ready for anything and equal to anything through Him Who infuses inner strength into me; I am self-sufficient in Christ's sufficiency].
Philippians 4:13 AMP

God's Ability

Andrew Murray

Those who seek to live like Christ must also relinquish ourselves to God, that we might learn to be and do nothing but his will. Realizing that we have not the ability to think or do anything good or holy within our own power, we must be willing to submit every faculty of body, soul, and spirit to Jesus.

The distrust of self in everything and the trust of Jesus in everything are what enable us to do the will of God. Then the very spirit of the cross breathes through our whole being.

 *call heaven and earth to record this day against you, that I have set before you life and death, blessing and cursing: therefore choose life, that both thou and thy seed may live."*

Deuteronomy 30:19 KJV

62

*H*ow foolish—even mad—it is for one with understanding to prefer deliberately temporal things to eternal. How contrary to all reason to prefer the happiness of a year to the happiness of eternity, for there cannot be any medium between everlasting joy and everlasting pain.

—John Wesley

Amazing Grace

Charles Spurgeon

Observe the rain that drops from heaven. It falls on the desert as well as on the fertile field. It drops on the rock that will refuse its fertilizing moisture as well as on the soil that opens its gaping mouth to drink it in with gratitude. See, it falls on the hard-trodden streets of the populous city, where it is not required and where men will even curse it for coming. It falls no more freely where the sweet flowers have been panting for it and the withering leaves have been rustling forth their prayers.

Such is the grace of God. It does not visit us because we ask for it, much less because we deserve it. But as God wills it, the bottles of heaven are unstopped and grace descends. No matter how vile and black and foul and godless men may be, he will have mercy on whom he will have mercy. That free, rich, overflowing goodness of his can make the very worst and least deserving the objects of his best and choicest love.

 *eeply respect* GOD, *your God.*
Serve and worship Him
exclusively.

Deuteronomy 6:13 MSG

*W*orship is giving God the best that he has given you. Be careful what you do with the best you have. Whenever you get a blessing from God, give it back to him as a love gift. Take time to meditate before God and offer the blessing back to him in a deliberate act of worship.

—Oswald Chambers

*T*o worship God in spirit and truth means to worship God as we ought to worship him. God is Spirit, so we must worship him in spirit and truth, that is, by a humble and true adoration of spirit in the depth and center of our souls. God alone can see this worship; we can repeat it so often that in the end it becomes as if it were natural to us, and as if God were one with our souls, and our souls one with him.

—Brother Lawrence

*T*he most valuable thing the Psalms do for me is to express that same delight in God which made David dance.

—C. S. Lewis

*M*y worth to God in public is what I am in private.
—Oswald Chambers

If any man has a hundred sheep, and one of them has gone astray, does he not leave the ninety-nine on the mountains and go and search for the one that is straying? If it turns out that he finds it, truly I say to you, he rejoices over it more than over the ninety-nine which have not gone astray. So it is not the will of your Father who is in heaven that one of these little ones perish."

Matthew 18:12–14 NASB

Accept Your Worth

John G. Lake

At what point do we start thinking of our worth through his eyes? If it's true that the value of something is measured by what someone else will pay, then we need to rethink our worth. Do we ever acknowledge who we are before him? Please don't misunderstand, I'm not encouraging arrogance or cockiness. But wouldn't it honor him more if we believed that he actually did a good enough job in saving us, and that we really are saved?

...Doesn't it honor him more when his children no longer see themselves only as sinners saved by grace, but now as heirs of God?

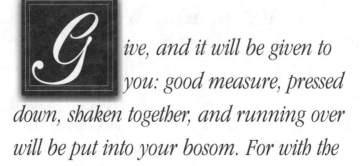 *ive, and it will be given to you: good measure, pressed down, shaken together, and running over will be put into your bosom. For with the same measure that you use, it will be measured back to you.*

Luke 6:38 NKJV

*G*race binds you with far stronger cords than the cords of duty or obligation can bind you. Grace is free, but when once you take it you are bound forever to the giver, and bound to catch the spirit of the giver. Like produces like, grace makes you gracious, the giver makes you give.

—E. Stanley Jones

God in a Box?

J. B. Phillips

The man who is outside all organized Christianity may have, and often does have, a certain reverence for God, and a certain genuine respect for Jesus Christ. But what sticks in his throat about the Christianity of the Churches is not merely their differences in denomination, but the spirit of "churchiness" which seems to pervade them all. They seem to him to have captured and tamed and trained to their own liking. Something that is really far too big ever to be forced into little man-made boxes with neat labels upon them. He may never think of putting it into words, but this is what he thinks and feels.

"If," the churches appear to be saying to him, "you will jump through our particular hoop or sign on our particular dotted line, then we will introduce you to God. But if not, then there's no God for you." This seems to him to be nonsense, and nasty arrogant nonsense at that.... If God is God, he's BIG, and generous and magnificent, and I can't see that anybody can say they've made a 'corner' in God, or shut him up in their particular box.

*od is faithful through whom
you were called into fellowship
with his Son, Jesus Christ our Lord.*

1 Corinthians 1:9 NASB

In a Christian community, everything depends upon whether each individual is an indispensable link in a chain. Only when even the smallest link is securely interlocked is the chain unbreakable.

—Dietrich Bonhoeffer

One hundred worshipers [meeting] together, each one looking away to Christ, are in heart nearer to each other than they could possibly be, were they to become 'unity' conscious and turn their eyes away from God to strive for closer fellowship.

—A. W. Tozer

It is the part of a Christian to take care of his own body for the very purpose that by its soundness and well-being he may be enabled to labor... thus the stronger member may serve the weaker member, and we may be children of God, and busy for one another, bearing one another's burdens, and so fulfilling the law of Christ.

—Martin Luther

*C*hrist is our temple, in whom by faith all believers meet.
—Matthew Henry

*L*et the peace of God rule in your hearts, to which also you were called
in one body; and be thankful.

Colossians 3:15 NKJV

One Heart—One Soul

Matthew Henry

The seat of Christian unity is in the heart or spirit: it does not lie in one set of thoughts, nor in one form and mode of worship, but in one heart and one soul. This unity of heart and affection may be said to be of the Spirit of God; it is wrought by him, and is one of the fruits of the Spirit. This we should endeavour to keep. Endeavouring is a gospel word. We must do our utmost.

 *herefore encourage one another and build each other up.*

1 Thessalonians 5:11 NIV

*I*n God, we live every commonplace as well as the most exalted moment of our being. To trust in him when no need is pressing, when things seem going right of themselves, may be harder than when things seem going wrong.

—George MacDonald

A Ray of Truth

Henry Drummond

I had an egg for breakfast this morning, and I saw that it was an egg; there it was, shell and all. God made that egg. I had an egg for dinner today, but it was in the pudding, and it didn't look in the least like an egg, but it did me just as much good as the egg which I had for breakfast and which I saw with my eyes.

You get a ray of truth through a book, or a man, or a picture, or a tree, or the sky; it doesn't matter the form of it if it does you good, if it inspires you and draws you near to God.

Don't be suspicious of it if it is God's truth, even if its form changes. In talking to a man—if you are to win him in that way—talk in the man's own language if you can. But I was going to say more particularly that one has to do a great deal more to display and live out his Christianity than merely to talk to people about religion.

f anyone wants to be first,
he shall be last of all and
servant of all."

Mark 9:35 NASB

*H*e who waits to do a great deal of good at once will never do anything.
—Samuel Johnson

*I*n taking the form of a servant, Jesus established the law of rank in the church of
Christ. The higher one wishes to stand in grace, the more it must be
his joy to be a servant of all.
—Andrew Murray

*D*o all the good you can, by all the means you can, in all the ways you can,
in all the places you can, at all the times you can, to all the people you can,
as long as ever you can.
—John Wesley

We sometimes fear to bring our troubles to God, because they must seem small to him who sitteth on the circle of the earth. But if they are large enough to vex and endanger our welfare, they are large enough to touch his heart of love. For love does not measure by a merchant's scales, not with a surveyor's chain. It hath a delicacy... unknown in any handling of material substance.

—R. A. Torrey

In the world you will have tribulation; but be of good cheer,
I have overcome the world."
John 16:33 NKJV

Comfort During Difficult Times

Charles Spurgeon

During all times when your spirit is downcast and discouraged, hurry to the Lord Jesus Christ. Whenever the cares of this life burden you and your way seems hard for your weary feet, hurry to your Father in heaven. There may be other sources of consolation, but they will not at all times restore you—and certainly not with as much power and assurance.

In God, however, there dwells such a fullness of comfort.... When you do so, you will find that he strengthens the hands that hang down and fortifies the feeble knees.

*o temptation has seized you except what is common to man. And God is faithful; he will not let you be tempted beyond what you can bear. But when you are tempted, he will also provide a way out so that you can stand up under it.*

1 Corinthians 10:13 NIV

$\mathcal{I}$f we do not abide in prayer, we will abide in temptation. Let this be one aspect of our daily intercession: "God, preserve my soul, and keep my heart and all its ways so that I will not be entangled." When this is true in our lives, a passing temptation will not overcome us. We will remain free while others lie in bondage.

—John Owen

Absolutely All

R. A. Torrey

The miracle of the five loaves and two fishes (Matt. 14:17–20), is deeply significant. The disciples said unto Jesus, "We have here but five loaves, and two fishes." He said, "Bring them hither to me."

We are told with a good deal of emphasis upon the definite article, he "took THE five loaves and THE two fishes," that is, he took all that they had. It was not much, but they brought it all. Then he blessed it and broke it and there was an abundance for all.

But if one of these insignificant barley loaves had been kept back, or one of these little fishes, there would not have been enough to go around....

...Here lies the secret of failure in many a one who would work for Christ; there is one cracker kept back, or one little fish. We talk very lightly of absolute surrender to God, but it means more than most people who profess it seem to realize. I would ask each reader of these pages, have you brought all to Christ—absolutely all—absolutely ALL.

o not worry, saying, 'What shall we eat?' or 'What shall we drink?' or 'What shall we wear?' ...For your heavenly Father knows that you need all these things."

Matthew 6:31–32 NKJV

*B*e not miserable about what may happen tomorrow. The same everlasting Father,
who cares for you today, will care for you tomorrow.

—Francis de Sales

*O*ur anxiety does not empty tomorrow of its sorrow, but only
empties today of its strength.

—Charles Spurgeon

*I*n almost everything that touches our everyday life on earth, God is pleased when
we're pleased. He wills that we be as free as birds to soar and sing
our maker's praise without anxiety.

—A. W. Tozer

I would maintain that thanks are the highest form of thought, and that gratitude is happiness doubled by wonder.

—G. K. Chesterton

Happy are the people whose God is the Lord!
Psalm 144:15 NKJV

Happiness of the Soul

George Müller

In what way shall we attain to this settled happiness of soul? How shall we learn to enjoy God? How shall we obtain such an all-sufficient soul-satisfying portion in him as shall enable us to let go the things of this world as vain and worthless in comparison?

I answer, "This happiness is to be obtained through the study of the Holy Scriptures. God has therein revealed himself unto us in the face of Jesus Christ."

 f you listen to constructive
criticism, you will be at
home among the wise.

Proverbs 15:3 NLT

*C*riticism may not be agreeable, but it is necessary. It fulfils the same function as pain in the human body. It calls attention to an unhealthy state of things.

—Winston Churchill

The Spirit of God Within

William Law

The scripture saith, "We are not sufficient of ourselves to think a good thought." If so, then we cannot be chargeable with not thinking and willing that which is good but upon this supposition, that there is always a supernatural power within us, ready and able to help us to the good which we cannot have from ourselves.

The difference then of a good and a bad man does not lie in this, that the one wills that which is good, and the other does not, but solely in this, that the one concurs with the living inspiring Spirit of God within him and the other resists it, and is and can be only chargeable with evil because he resists it.

Therefore whether you consider that which is good or bad in a man, they equally prove the perpetual indwelling and operation of the Spirit of God within us since we can only be bad by resisting, as we are good by yielding to the Spirit of God, both which equally suppose a perpetual operation of the Spirit of God within us.

*et the peace of Christ rule in your hearts, since as members of one body you were called to peace.*

Colossians 3:15 NIV

First keep the peace within yourself, then you can also bring peace to others.
—Thomas à Kempis

Christ's life outwardly was one of the most troubled lives that was ever lived: tempest and tumult, tumult and tempest, the waves breaking over it all the time. But the inner life was a sea of glass. The great calm was always there.
—Henry Drummond

Man is not at peace with his fellow man because he is not at peace with himself; he is not at peace with himself, because he is not at peace with God.
—Thomas Merton

*H*ave patience with all things, but chiefly have patience with yourself. Do not lose courage in considering your own imperfections but instantly set about remedying them—every day begin the task anew.

—Francis de Sales

*B*ut if we hope for what is still unseen by us, we wait for it with patience and composure.

Romans 8:25 AMP

Perfecting Patience

John Wesley

There is no love of God without patience, and no patience without lowliness and sweetness of spirit.

Humility and patience are the surest proofs of the increase of love.

Humility alone unites patience with love; without which it is impossible to draw profit from suffering; or indeed, to avoid complaint, especially when we think we have given no occasion for what men make us suffer.

True humility is a kind of self-annihilation; and this is the center of all virtues.

A soul returned to God ought to be attentive to everything which is said to him, on the head of salvation, with a desire to profit thereby.

ut be ye doers of the word, and not hearers only, deceiving your own selves. For if any be a hearer of the word, and not a doer, he is like unto a man beholding his natural face in a glass: for he beholdeth himself, and goeth his way, and straightway forgetteth what manner of man he was. But whoso looketh into the perfect law of liberty, and continueth therein, he being not a forgetful hearer, but a doer of the work, this man shall be blessed in his deed.

James 1:22–25 KJV

Practical obedience naturally follows the subject of practical faith. Trust and obey are the two wings which maintain the equilibrium of our flight, the two oars which keep us steadily in the channel of our course.

—A. B. Simpson

God's Purpose for Men
E. M. Bounds

We are constantly on a stretch, if not on a strain, to devise new methods, new plans, new organizations to advance the Church and secure enlargement and efficiency for the gospel. This trend of the day has a tendency to lose sight of the man, or sink the man in the plan or organization. God's plan is to make much of the man, far more of him than of anything else. Men are God's method. The Church is looking for better methods; God is looking for better men....

When Paul appeals to the personal character of the men who rooted the gospel in the world, he solves the mystery of their success. The glory and efficiency of the gospel is staked on the men who proclaim it. When God declares that "the eyes of the Lord run to and fro throughout the whole earth, to show himself strong in the behalf of them whose heart is perfect toward him," he declares the necessity of men and his dependence on them as a channel through which to exert his power upon the world.

 o be strong and take courage, all you who put your hope in the LORD!

Psalm 31:24 NLT

*E*xpect great things from God; attempt great things for God.
—William Carey

*C*ourage is not simply one of the virtues, but the form of every
virtue at the testing point.
—C. S. Lewis

*C*ourage is rightly esteemed the first of human qualities ... because it is
the quality which guarantees all others.
—Winston Churchill

Train yourself to recognize the hand of God in everything that happens to you.

—Andrew Murray

In this you greatly rejoice, though now for a little while, if need be, you have been grieved by various trials, that the genuineness of your faith... may be found to praise, honor, and glory at the revelation of Jesus Christ.

1 Peter 1:6–7 NKJV

God—Our Defender

D. L. Moody

Many a young believer is discouraged and disheartened when he thinks the odds are against him. He begins to believe God has forsaken him, that Christianity is not all that it professes to be. But he should rather regard it as an encouraging sign....The fiercest attacks are made on the strongest forts, and the fiercer the battle the young believer is called on to wage, the surer evidence it is that the Holy Spirit in working his heart. God will not desert him in his time of need.

 press on toward the goal for the prize of the upward call of God in Christ Jesus.

Philippians 3:14 NASB

Dreams are true while they last, and do we not live in dreams?
—Alfred Lord Tennyson

Contentment of Heart

Thomas Watson

Advance faith. All our disquiets do issue immediately from unbelief. It is this that raiseth the storm of discontent in the heart. O set faith a-work! It is the property of faith to silence our doubtings, to scatter our fears, to still the heart when the passions are up. Faith works the heart to a sweet serene composure; it is not having food and raiment, but having faith, which will make us content. Faith chides down passion; when reason begins to sink, let faith swim.

Faith shows the soul that whatever its trials are yet it is from the hand of a father; it is indeed a bitter cup, but "shall I not drink the cup which my father hath given me to drink?"

It is in love to my soul: God corrects me with the same love he crowns me; God is now training me up for heaven; he carves me, to make me a polished shaft. These sufferings bring forth patience, humility, even the peaceful fruits of righteousness. And if God can bring such sweet fruit out of our stock, let him graft me where he pleases. Thus faith brings the heart to holy contentment.

*W*hoever wants to be a leader among you must be your servant.

Matthew 20:26 NLT

*G*oodness makes greatness truly valuable, and greatness make goodness much more serviceable.

—Matthew Henry

*N*o one ever became great except through many and great mistakes.

—William E. Gladstone

*G*od does not call those who are equipped, he equips those whom he has called.

—Smith Wigglesworth

*T*rust the past to God's mercy, the present to God's love and the future to God's providence.

—St. Augustine

*T*rust in the LORD with all your heart, and lean not on your own understanding.

Proverbs 3:5 NKJV

When Our Help Ends, God's Help Begins

Martin Luther

When we see no way or means, by advice or aid, through which we may be helped in our miseries, we at once conclude, according to our human reason: now our condition is desperate; but when we believe trustingly in God, our deliverance begins.

The physician says: Where philosophy ends, physic begins; so we say: Where human help is at an end, God's help begins, or faith in God's Word. Trials and temptations appear before deliverance, after deliverance comes joy. To be suppressed and troubled, is to arise, to grow and to increase.

*here is a time for everything,
and a season for every
activity under heaven.*

Ecclesiastes 3:1 NIV

The wise and diligent traveler watches his every step, and always has his eyes upon the part of the road directly in front of him. But he does not turn constantly backward to count every step, and to examine every track. He would lose time in going forward.

—François Fénelon

Fact! Faith! Feeling!

F. B. Meyer

These three words stand for three most important factors in character and life. We all have to do with them in one form or another, but it is above all things necessary that we should place them in the right order.

Most people try to put Feeling first, with as much success as if they tried to build the top storey of a house before laying its foundations. Their order is—

- Feeling or Fact
- Fact or Faith
- Faith or Fact

Others seek Faith first, without considering the Facts on which alone Faith and Feeling can rest. They resemble a man who, desiring to get warm on a frosty night, refuses to approach the fire which burns brightly on the hearth.

The only possible order that will bring blessing and comfort to the heart is that indicated in our title.

God's Facts, laid like a foundation of adamant.

Our Faith, apprehending, and resting on them.

Joyous Feeling, coming, it may be, at once, or after the lapse of days and months, as God will.

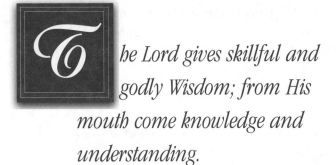 he Lord gives skillful and
godly Wisdom; from His
mouth come knowledge and
understanding.

Proverbs 2:6 AMP

*I*f ye keep watch over your hearts, and listen for the voice of God and learn of him, in one short hour ye can learn more from him than ye could learn from man in a thousand years.

—Johannes Tauler

*K*nowledge comes, but wisdom lingers.

—Alfred Lord Tennyson

*A*bove all, believe confidently that Jesus delights in maintaining that new nature within you, and imparting to it his strength and wisdom for its work.

—Andrew Murray

The unthankful heart... discovers no mercies; but let the thankful heart sweep
through the day and, as the magnet finds the iron, so it will find,
in every hour, some heavenly blessings!

—Henry Ward Beecher

*Just as you received Christ Jesus as Lord, continue to live in him, rooted and
built up in him, strengthened in the faith as you were taught,
and overflowing with thankfulness.*

Colossians 2:6–7 NIV

With Thankfulness

Charles Spurgeon

As a father cares deeply for his children, so God cares deeply for you. Oh, the breadth of the love of Christ! Shall such a love as this receive half our hearts? Shall it receive a cold love in return? Shall Jesus' marvelous lovingkindness and tender care receive only faint response and lukewarm acknowledgment?

O my soul, tune your harp to a glad song of thanksgiving! Go to your rest rejoicing, for you are no isolated wanderer, but a beloved child, watched over, cared for, supplied, and defended by your Lord.

Topical Index

Index of Names

Additional copies of this and other
Honor products are available wherever good books are sold.

If you have enjoyed this book,
or if it has had an impact on your life,
we would like to hear from you.

Please contact us at:

Honor Books
Cook Communications Ministries, Dept. 201
4050 Lee Vance View
Colorado Springs, CO 80918
Or visit our Web site:
www.cookministries.com

HONOR **HB** BOOKS

Inspiration and Motivation for the Seasons of Life